Axel Jørgensen

ROMANCE
for Trombone and Piano

Op. 21

First performance:
Wednesday 28th June, 1916, at the Tivoli Concert Hall, Denmark

Solo trombonist:
Anton Hansen, The Royal Danish Orchestra, Copenhagen

Edition Wilhelm Hansen AS, Copenhagen

Axel Jorgensen (1881-1947)
A Biographical Profile

by Per Gade

Born: Skiveholme Terp, close to Aarhus town. Died: Copenhagen.

Jorgensen spent most of his childhood in Skanderborg town, where his father was Director of Music. When he was a boy he played the tenorhorn and violin. At only 16 years of age, he was accepted by the entrance examination to the Royal Academy of Music in Copenhagen, and was given a scholarship to study free because he demonstrated exceptional talent for music. Here he studied violin and composition. In 1916 he became a member of Tivoli Concert Hall Orchestra in Copenhagen. He also spent some time in Paris, France as an orchestra player before he returned to Denmark again, where be became a member of the Royal Opera & Ballet House Orchestra as a viola player.

As a composer he is probably best remembered today for his pieces for trombone and piano, and his *Brass Quintet* (for 5 valve instruments). Jorgensen's good friend was the legendary Danish trombone-virtuoso, Anton Hansen. They both played together since their early years, first in Tivoli and later in the Royal Orchestra. It was because of the influence of Anton Hansen's solo trombone performances that today we have several compositions for brass instruments by Axel Jorgensen, representing this period in Danish music life.

His *Romance for Trombone and Piano* had its first performance in 1916 by Anton Hansen, who played it with an arrangement for orchestra. (This arrangement was later lost in the conflagration of Tivoli Concert Hall during the last world war). A few years later the version for trombone and piano came out in its first print in Paris by Evette & Schaeffer in 1921.

ISBN 87 7455 504 9

Romance

for
Trombone and Piano

Axel Jørgensen, op. 21
(1881 - 1947)

Editor : Per Gade

Axel Jørgensen

ROMANCE

for Trombone and Piano

Edition Wilhelm Hansen AS, Copenhagen

Trombone

Romance

for
Trombone and Piano

Axel Jørgensen, op. 21
(1881 - 1947)

Editor: Per Gade

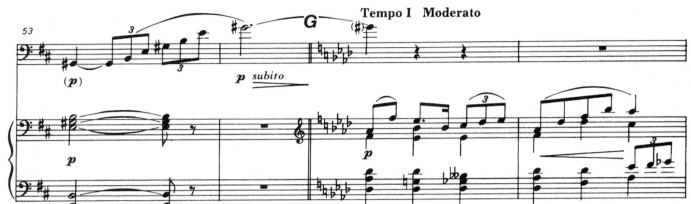